NATIONAL
GEOGRAPHIC
KiDS

weird but true!

SHARKS

weird but true!

SHARKS

300
FIN-NOMENAL
FACTS TO DIVE INTO

NATIONAL GEOGRAPHIC
WASHINGTON, D.C.

In the 16th century, sailors referred to sharks as sea dogs.

Ahoy, matey!

Shark egg cases are also known as mermaid purses.

4

CAN PICK UP THE SOUND OF INJURED PREY MORE THAN A MILE (1.6 KM) AWAY.

Shark skin is made of **dermal denticles,** or "skin teeth."

Bull sharks sometimes headbutt fish before eating them.

5

A whale shark's SPOT PATTERN

is as **UNIQUE** as a **HUMAN'S FINGERPRINT.**

Yummy!

A POD OF ORCAS WILL SOMETIMES ATTACK A GREAT WHITE SHARK AND EAT ONLY ITS LIVER.

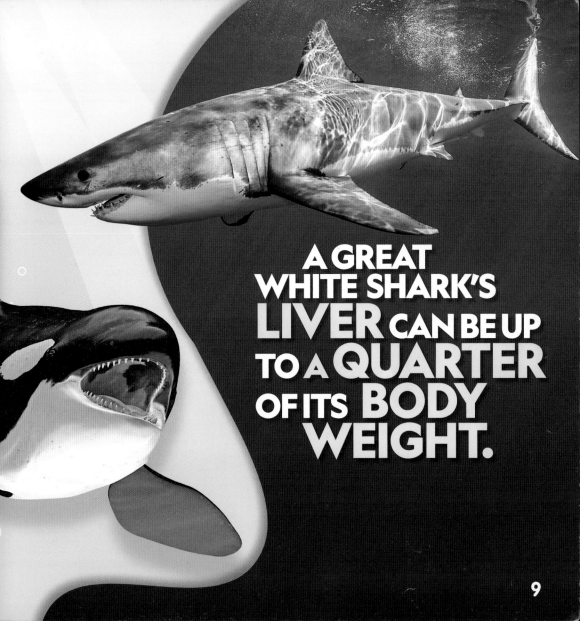

A GREAT WHITE SHARK'S LIVER CAN BE UP TO A QUARTER OF ITS BODY WEIGHT.

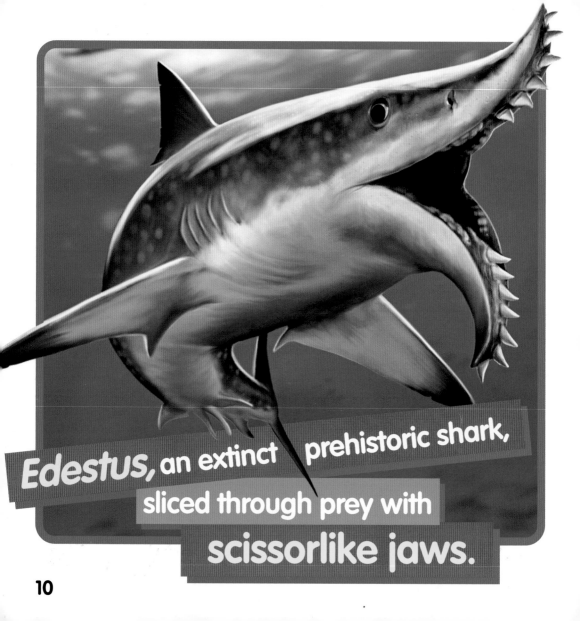

Edestus, an extinct prehistoric shark, sliced through prey with scissorlike jaws.

A Port Jackson shark mother screws her SPIRAL-SHAPED EGG CASE into rocks with her MOUTH.

The black TENDRILS that hang from the egg case get TANGLED IN SEAWEED to anchor it further.

11

WALKING SHARKS use their fins to WALK ON THE SEAFLOOR and even briefly ABOVE WATER on coral reefs.

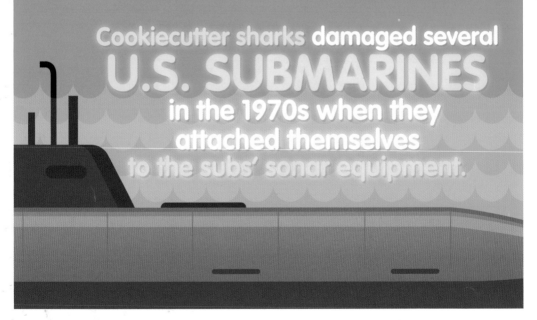

Cookiecutter sharks damaged several U.S. SUBMARINES in the 1970s when they attached themselves to the subs' sonar equipment.

A hammerhead shark's **nostrils,** just like **its eyes,** are located on either side of **its head.**

PYJAMA SHARKS ARE NAMED FOR THEIR **STRIPED BODIES** THAT LOOK LIKE PJ'S.

GOBLIN SHARKS ARE PINK.

Sharks don't blink.

TIGER SHARKS have been found with **LICENSE PLATES** and **TIRES** in their **STOMACHS.**

More than half of a **bonnethead shark's** diet is **seagrass.**

Cookiecutter sharks use their sharp teeth to attach themselves to their prey and cut out a cookie-shaped chunk of flesh.

Only about **5 PERCENT** of shark species can live in **FRESHWATER.**

VIPER DOGFISH, A TYPE OF DEEP-SEA SHARK, USE THEIR EXTENDABLE JAWS TO SNATCH PREY.

Female sharks can have skin that is **two times thicker** than **male sharks'**.

Greenland sharks sometimes eat land animals like horses and reindeer that fall through the ice into the ocean.

Uh-oh.

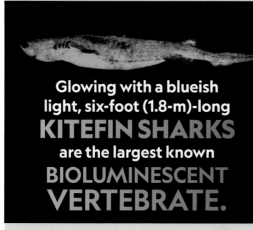

Glowing with a blueish light, six-foot (1.8-m)-long **KITEFIN SHARKS** are the largest known **BIOLUMINESCENT VERTEBRATE.**

Part of a shark's intestines are **CORKSCREW-SHAPED.**

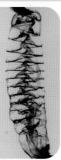

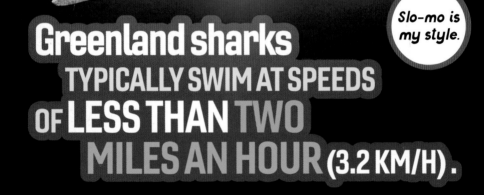

Greenland sharks TYPICALLY SWIM AT SPEEDS OF **LESS THAN** TWO MILES AN HOUR (3.2 KM/H).

Slo-mo is my style.

Gray reef sharks form friendships that can last for years.

Hammerheads use their **hammer-shaped heads** to pin stingrays to the **ocean floor** before **eating them.**

21

SAW SHARKS HAVE **SAWLIKE SNOUTS,** WHICH THEY USE TO SLASH AT PREY.

PARASITES attach to and feed on **GREENLAND SHARKS' EYES,** leaving many of them with **POOR VISION.**

23

WOBBEGONG SHARKS lie still on the ocean floor and then **SUCK UP PASSING PREY** whole with their **VACUUM-LIKE MOUTHS.**

BEARD-LIKE LOBES around their mouths help lure fish and CRUSTACEANS.

Whitetip reef sharks poke their heads into coral reef crevices and z-z-z snatch **SLEEPING OCTOPUSES.**

In 2012, researchers studied **A 10-FOOT (3-m)-LONG** female bull shark nicknamed **BIG BLUE** that weighed about as much as a **GRAND PIANO.**

TIGER SHARKS HAVE SERRATED TEETH THAT CAN CUT THROUGH **TURTLE SHELLS.**

EACH SCALE on a shark's skin is about **THE SAME WIDTH AS** A FEW **HUMAN HAIRS.**

LEOPARD SHARKS SUCK OUT innkeeper worms FROM THEIR BURROWS to eat them.

The sharks have been found with bite marks **from the worms** inside their mouths.

A female whale shark can give birth to as many as **300 pups.**

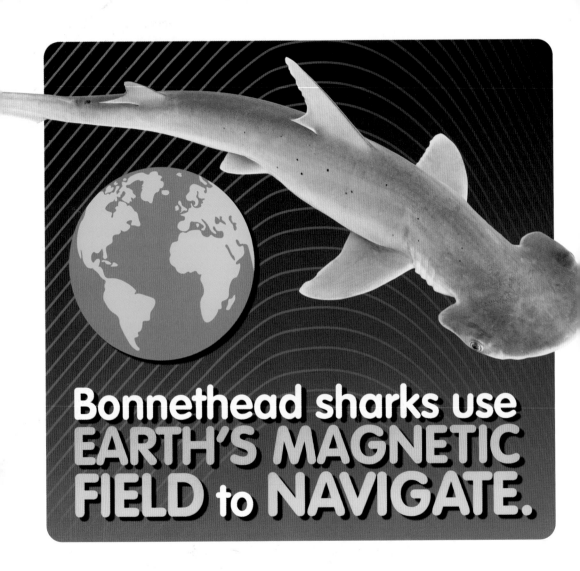

Bonnethead sharks use **EARTH'S MAGNETIC FIELD** to **NAVIGATE.**

Peter Benchley, the author of the 1974 novel **JAWS,** has a species of shark named after him: *Etmopterus benchleyi.*

Porbeagles, a type of mackerel shark, **play—they roll in kelp** and **push floating objects.**

MOST SHARKS CAN SEE IN COLOR.

Porbeagle sharks have been seen **chasing each** other in what looks like **a game of tag.**

PACIFIC OCEAN

NORTH AMERICA

ASIA

INDIAN OCEAN

AUSTRALIA

OCEANIA

PACIFIC OCEAN

SOUTH AMERICA

Shark sanctuaries in the Pacific Ocean cover an area that is TWO TIMES THE SIZE OF EUROPE.

MAP KEY
- Size of Europe*
- Size of shark sanctuaries in the Pacific Ocean

*Europe is placed on top of the shark sanctuaries to show the size comparision. This isn't the location of the continent.

0   2,000 miles

0   2,000 kilometers

Some sharks grow a new set of teeth EVERY TWO WEEKS.

Scientists discovered that **tiger sharks** often prey on migrating land-based **songbirds** that fall in the sea during storms.

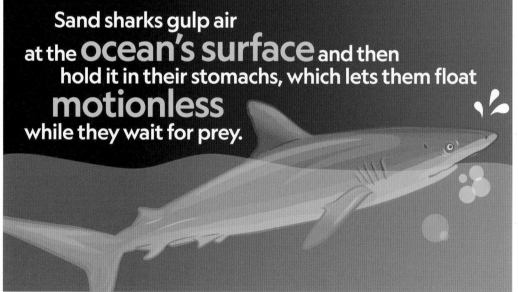

Sand sharks gulp air at the **ocean's surface** and then hold it in their stomachs, which lets them float **motionless** while they wait for prey.

Sharks swim in all of Earth's oceans.

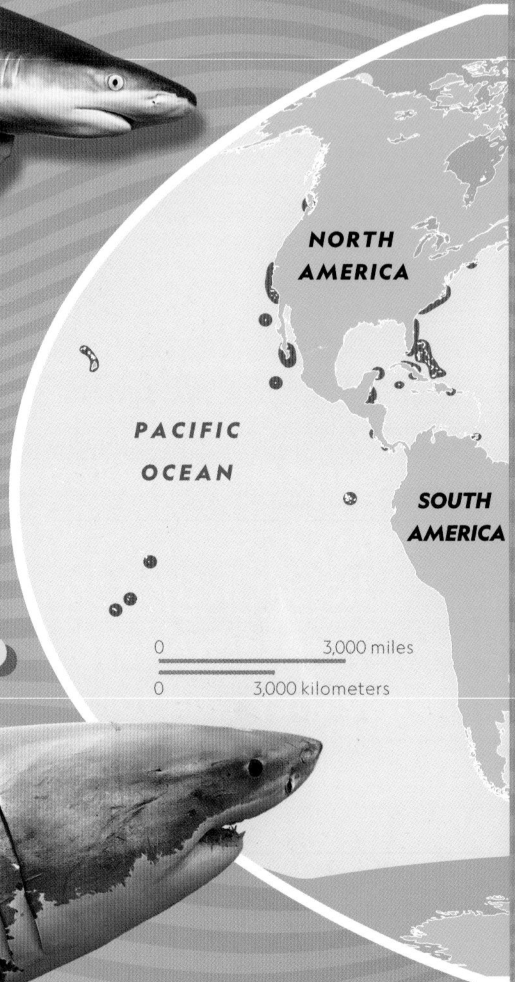

NORTH AMERICA

SOUTH AMERICA

PACIFIC OCEAN

0   3,000 miles

0   3,000 kilometers

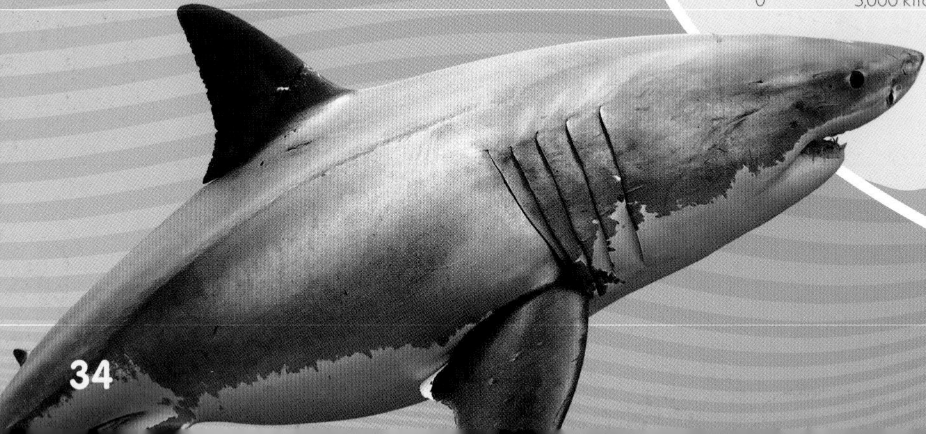

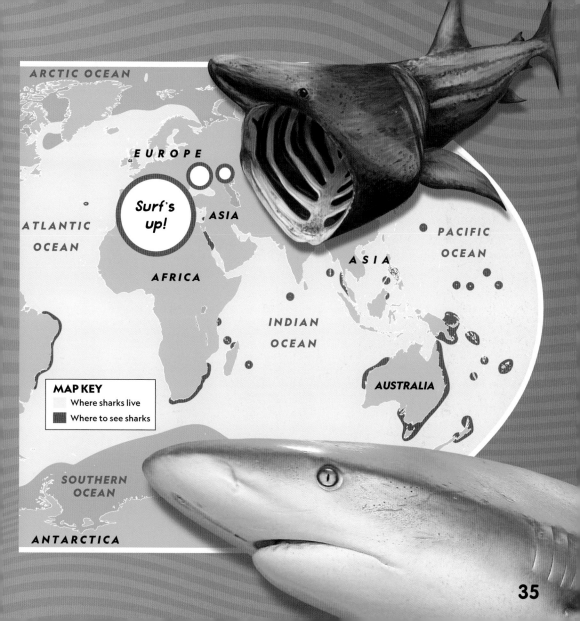

ARCTIC OCEAN

EUROPE

Surf's up!

ATLANTIC OCEAN

ASIA

AFRICA

ASIA

PACIFIC OCEAN

INDIAN OCEAN

AUSTRALIA

MAP KEY
Where sharks live
Where to see sharks

SOUTHERN OCEAN

ANTARCTICA

35

Great white sharks have only two predators: **orcas and humans.**

SCIENTISTS FOUND

TAPEWORM EGGS IN

270-MILLION-

YEAR-OLD FOSSILIZED

SHARK POOP.

37

Artist Spine B7 used **2,200** cans of **spray paint** to create a shark mural that is larger than **four basketball courts.**

Sharks survived **ALL FIVE OF EARTH'S MASS EXTINCTIONS.**

That's weird!

39

Sharks find food using

SPECIAL PORES ON THEIR SNOUTS,

which sense the electrical currents their prey give off.

Great white sharks **CHOMP** their prey, then shake it from side to side to **tear the flesh loose.**

SAND TIGER PUPS EAT EACH OTHER WHILE INSIDE THEIR MOTHER'S WOMB, LEAVING ONLY ONE PUP TO BE BORN.

A few **fossilized scales** from **450 million** years ago are the earliest evidence of sharklike animals.

We're BFFs!

Remora fish have a *suction cup–like* structure on *top of their heads* that help them *cling to sharks.*

When a shark finds something to eat, the remora **detaches itself** to **snack on the leftovers.**

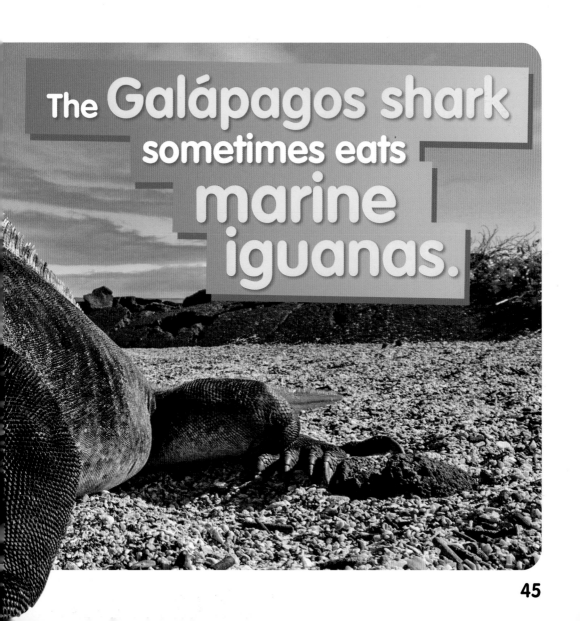

The **Galápagos shark** sometimes eats **marine iguanas.**

In Jupiter, Florida, U.S.A., people cheer for the **HAMMERHEADS,** a minor league baseball team whose mascot is Hamilton R. Head.

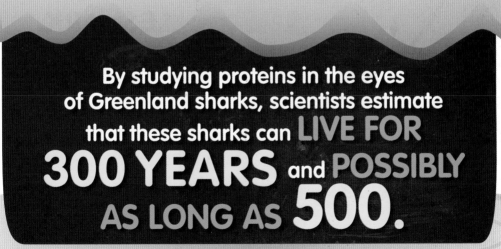

By studying proteins in the eyes of Greenland sharks, scientists estimate that these sharks can LIVE FOR 300 YEARS and POSSIBLY AS LONG AS 500.

The largest fish is

THE WHALE SHARK.

If a shark is **turned over on its back,** it goes into a relaxed, **trancelike state.**

There are more than

500 species

of shark.

MEGAMOUTH SHARKS
migrate every day:
They leave shallow water to
follow plankton,
their prey, to the deep sea
AT SUNSET.

The "Baby Shark" video has been viewed more than **11 billion** times.

The **Washington Nationals** went on a **winning streak after** outfielder Gerardo Parra chose it as his **walk-up** song in 2019.

Lemon shark skin looks **YELLOW** in shallow water, where these sharks live.

JULY 14 is **SHARK AWARENESS DAY.**

Frilled sharks have **25 rows** of backward-facing, trident-shaped teeth.

51

Scientists have spotted fewer than 50 GOBLIN SHARKS in the ocean.

FAST-SWIMMING SHORTFIN MAKOS ARE NICKNAMED "BLUE DYNAMITES."

In 2012, an inflatable shark nicknamed **CHOMPIE** "SWAM" through a building in Silver Spring, Maryland, U.S.A.

Megalodon ate 2,500 pounds (1,134 kg) of food a day—

BASKING SHARK MOMS GIVE BIRTH TO PUPS THAT ARE TALLER THAN THE AVERAGE 14-YEAR-OLD.

that's like you eating more than 20,000 hot dogs!

One of the earliest sharks, *Xenacanthus,* looked like an eel.

Scientists found that **BABY LEMON SHARKS** have **DISTINCT PERSONALITIES:** Some are **STANDOFFISH,** and others are **OUTGOING.**

You be you.

The prehistoric male ***Stethacanthus*** had a fin on its back shaped like an **ironing board.**

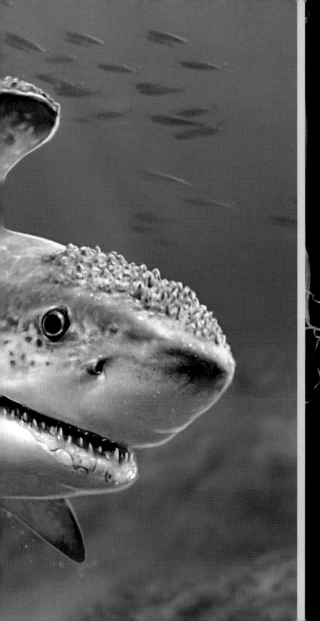

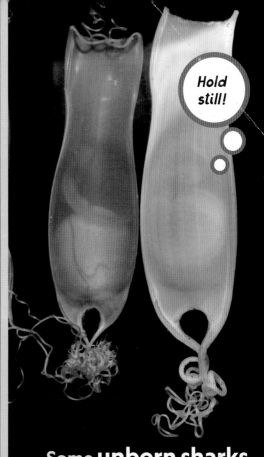

Some **unborn sharks** can sense danger and **stop moving in their egg case** so that predators don't **detect them.**

61

SHORTFIN MAKO SHARKS **CROSS UP TO** 2,485 MILES (4,000 KM) **OF OCEAN DURING THEIR** ANNUAL MIGRATIONS.

One man from Utah, U.S.A., has collected more than 800 rubber sharks.

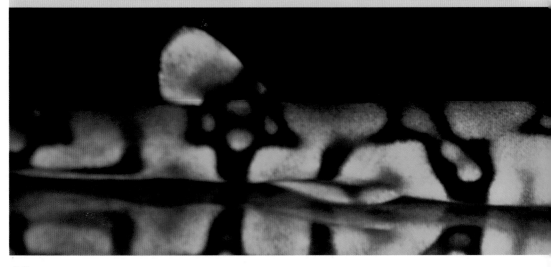

A marine robot called the **WasteShark** can gobble up about **16 tons (14.5 t)** of trash from the ocean each year.

Nom.
nom.
nom.

WASTESHARK

Cat sharks give off a **GREENISH LIGHT** to **COMMUNICATE** with each other, but it's invisible to **HUMANS.**

Red sea urchins, the main diet of horn sharks, **stain the** sharks' teeth **reddish brown.**

Sharks use their **inner ears** to **keep their balance—** just like **we do.**

The basking shark's common name comes from how it stays at the water's surface to **BASK,** or **SOAK,** in the **SUN.**

SHORTFIN MAKO SHARKS, the fastest sharks on Earth, chase prey in short bursts at

35 miles an hour

(56 km/h).

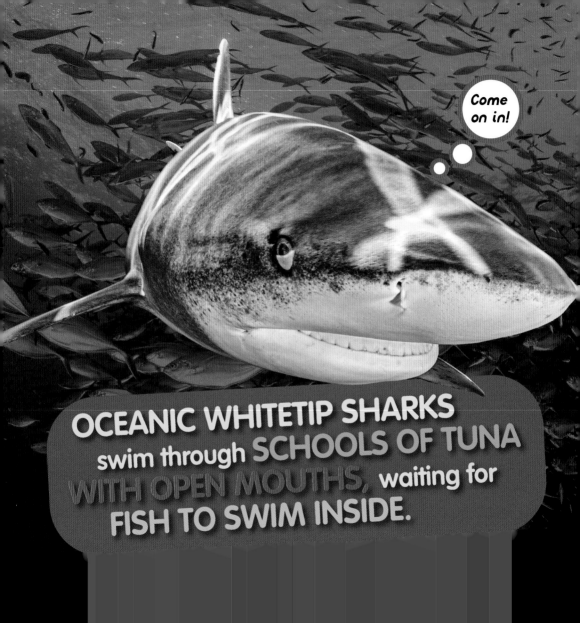

Nurse sharks partially bury themselves in the sand and breathe through openings behind their eyes.

"White Shark Café" is a large area in the Pacific Ocean where great white sharks migrate in the fall to feast.

Horn sharks' spines turn PURPLE when they eat a lot of purple sea urchins.

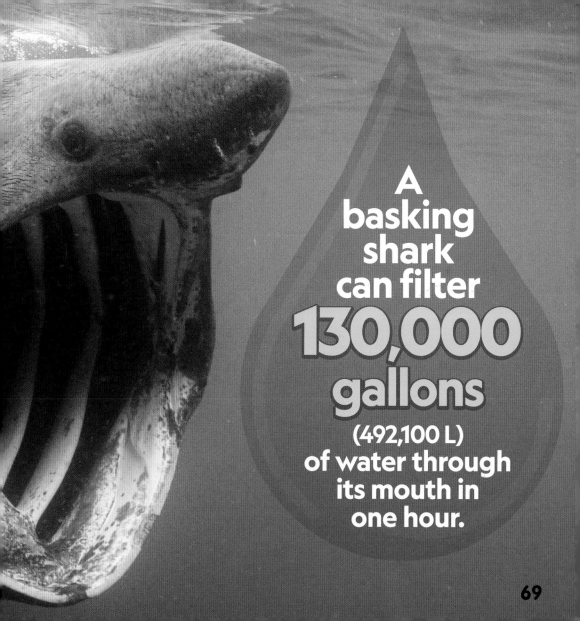

A
basking
shark
can filter
130,000
gallons
(492,100 L)
of water through
its mouth in
one hour.

SCIENTISTS HAVE FOUND **FOSSILIZED CROCODILE** POOP WITH SHARK TEETH MARKS IN IT.

The **extinct megalodon** was almost **three times longer** than a **great white shark.**

A shark's jaws aren't attached to its skull, allowing it to **THRUST ITS MOUTH FORWARD WHEN ATTACKING.**

71

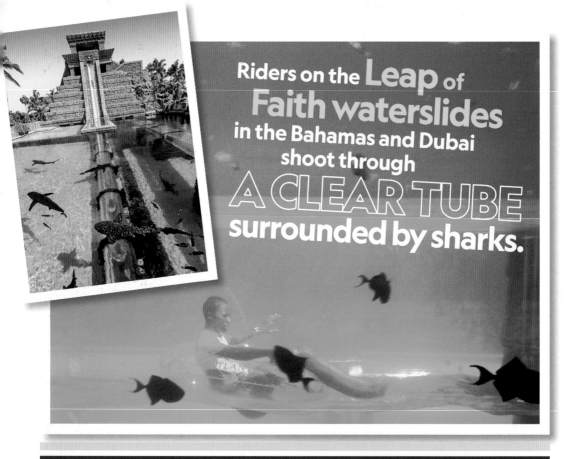

Riders on the **Leap** of **Faith** waterslides in the Bahamas and Dubai shoot through **A CLEAR TUBE** surrounded by sharks.

CROCODILE SHARKS repeatedly **SNAP THEIR JAWS** open and closed if **TAKEN OUT OF THE WATER.**

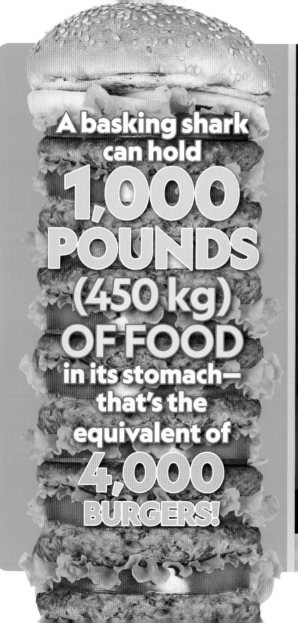

A basking shark can hold 1,000 POUNDS (450 kg) OF FOOD in its stomach—that's the equivalent of 4,000 BURGERS!

OCEANIC WHITETIP SHARKS ARE NICKNAMED THE "DARK KNIGHT OF THE OCEAN" BECAUSE THEY HUNT MOSTLY AT NIGHT.

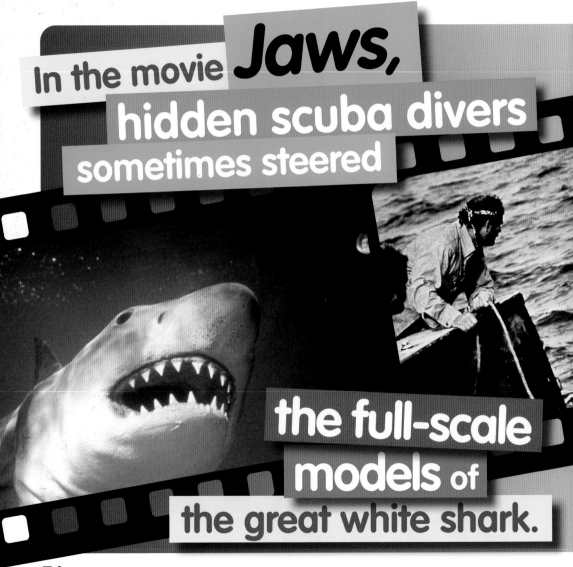

In the movie *Jaws,* hidden scuba divers sometimes steered the full-scale models of the great white shark.

The crew collectively nicknamed the trio of mechanical sharks BRUCE.

Galápagos sharks arch their backs and swim in figure eights to try to intimidate predators.

When pyjama sharks attack, they bite and then twist their prey's body in a maneuver called a **death roll.**

About two-thirds of a shark's brain is used for its sense of **smell.**

Sharks' **TEXTURED SKIN** makes them **RESISTANT** to barnacles and algae.

The United States Navy studied shark skin to make a material that **KEEPS BARNACLES** from attaching to **SHIP HULLS.**

77

Galápagos fur seals **hunt less frequently during full moons,** likely because the light makes them more visible to sharks.

Goliath groupers
prey on whitetip reef sharks, swallowing them whole.

Indigenous people in Brazil used shark teeth as **TOOLS,** which never had to be sharpened because shark teeth don't dull.

The state fossil of Georgia, U.S.A., is a **SHARK TOOTH.**

Researchers are studying **SHARKS' TAILS** to make better **UNDERWATER VEHICLES.**

Unlike other fish, sharks can **stiffen their tails mid-swish,** which creates twice as many **jets of water** and makes them **swim faster.**

SHARKS CAN **DETECT MOVEMENT IN COMPLETE DARKNESS.**

GREAT WHITE SHARKS CAN LEAP OUT OF THE WATER WHEN ATTACKING PREY.

One species of **frilled shark** has a **dorsal fin** that can look like **a horse's mane.**

A beachgoer has only a **one in 11.5 million chance** of being **bitten by a shark.**

Sharks spit out food they don't like.

83

Caribbean reef sharks *pile on top of one another* in caves, lying completely still for hours.

So cozy!

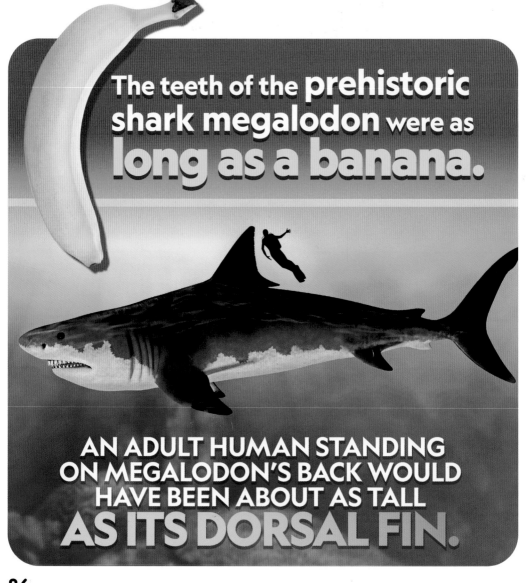

The teeth of the **prehistoric shark megalodon** were as **long as a banana.**

AN ADULT HUMAN STANDING ON MEGALODON'S BACK WOULD HAVE BEEN ABOUT AS TALL AS ITS DORSAL FIN.

FEMALE GREENLAND SHARKS DON'T REPRODUCE UNTIL THEY ARE ABOUT **150 YEARS OLD.**

I don't look a day over 149.

Bull sharks are rarely in aquarium exhibits—they'll eat the other fish.

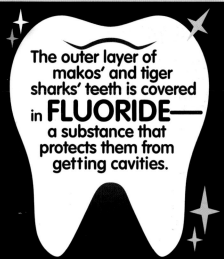

The outer layer of makos' and tiger sharks' teeth is covered in **FLUORIDE**— a substance that protects them from getting cavities.

SAW SHARKS are born with teeth that LIE FLAT AGAINST THEIR SNOUTS and later POP OUT to the sides.

AMERICAN ALLIGATORS sometimes attack LEMON, NURSE, and BONNETHEAD SHARKS.

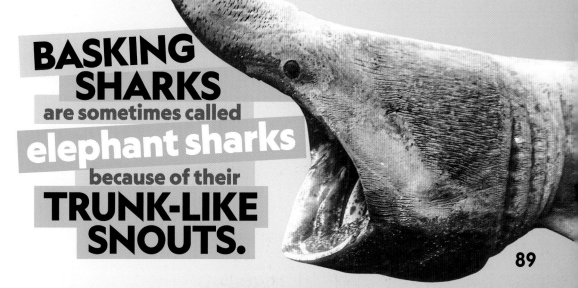

BASKING SHARKS are sometimes called **elephant sharks** because of their **TRUNK-LIKE SNOUTS.**

89

In the movie **Finding Dory,** **Destiny the whale shark** says she taught Dory to speak whale, but whale sharks are sharks, **not whales.**

Cat sharks stay in their egg cases for two years before emerging.

Great white sharks can detect a single drop of blood in the water from up to a third of a mile (.53 km) away.

Sevengill sharks use **comb-shaped teeth** on their lower jaws to **grab hold of prey** and jagged teeth on their upper jaws to **saw off flesh.**

Bull sharks will **slowly swim around remoras** to let them know they can **eat parasites** from the sharks' mouths, gills, and bodies.

Sharks can't **swim backward.**

93

ZEBRA SHARK PUPS ARE BORN WITH STRIPES THAT SLOWLY CHANGE TO DARK SPOTS.

Sharks can go more than a month without a big meal.

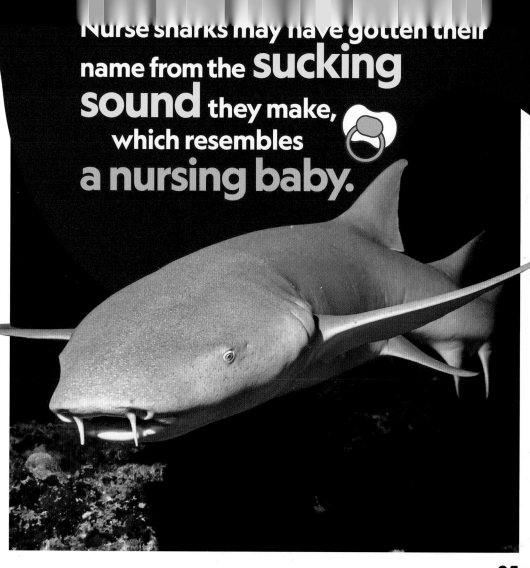

Nurse sharks may have gotten their name from the **sucking sound** they make, which resembles **a nursing baby.**

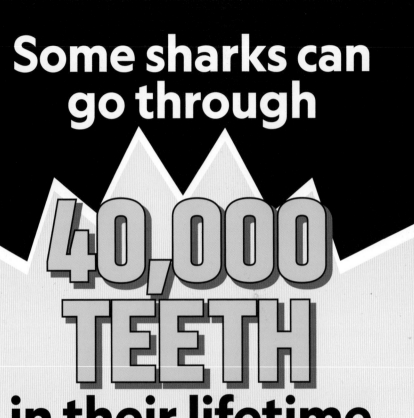

Some sharks can go through 40,000 TEETH in their lifetime.

To identify an individual whale shark by its unique pattern of spots, scientists use software that NASA developed to map the stars.

During the Middle Ages, people thought shark tooth fossils could **DETECT POISONS.**

THE 300-MILLION-YEAR-OLD *ORTHACANTHUS* SHARK SOMETIMES ATE ITS OWN YOUNG.

Dig me deeper.

SAWFISH—CLOSELY RELATED TO SHARKS—USE THEIR SAWLIKE JAWS TO RAKE THROUGH SAND TO FIND WORMS, SHRIMPS, AND CRABS TO EAT.

Some sharks push their stomachs out of their mouths to rinse them off.

Frilled sharks have **THICK SKIN FOLDS** along their bellies, which scientists think might **EXPAND TO HELP THEM DIGEST LARGER PREY.**

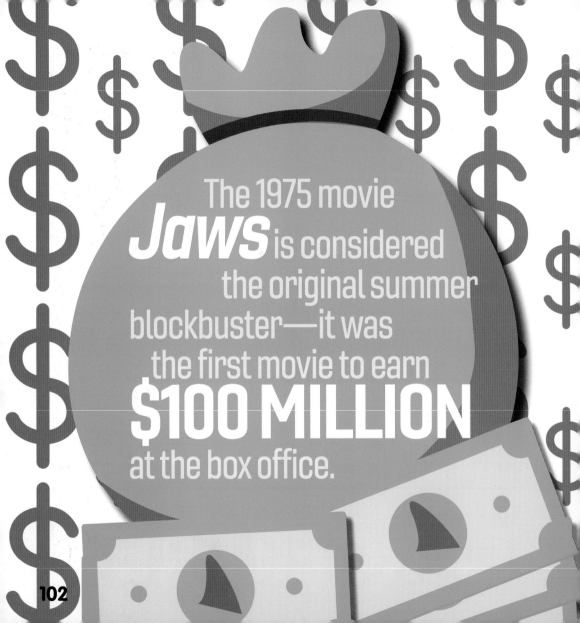

The 1975 movie *Jaws* is considered the original summer blockbuster—it was the first movie to earn **$100 MILLION** at the box office.

THREE ELITE MOUNTAIN CLIMBERS TOOK 12 DAYS TO CLIMB MERU PEAK IN INDIA BY SCALING A GRANITE WALL KNOWN AS **SHARK'S FIN.**

A 20-story apartment building SHAPED LIKE A SHARK FIN in Cancún, Mexico, includes a shark research lab.

#SharkTower

103

Who, me?

Cape fur seals attack and eat BLUE SHARKS.

A sand tiger shark's teeth **STICK OUT** of its mouth **even** when it's closed.

Some shark poop is spiral-shaped.

A SHARK'S STOMACH CONTAINS **ACIDS** STRONG ENOUGH TO **DISSOLVE** METAL.

The ancient shark **SQUALICORAX** snatched dinosaurs and pterosaurs that **FELL INTO THE WATER.**

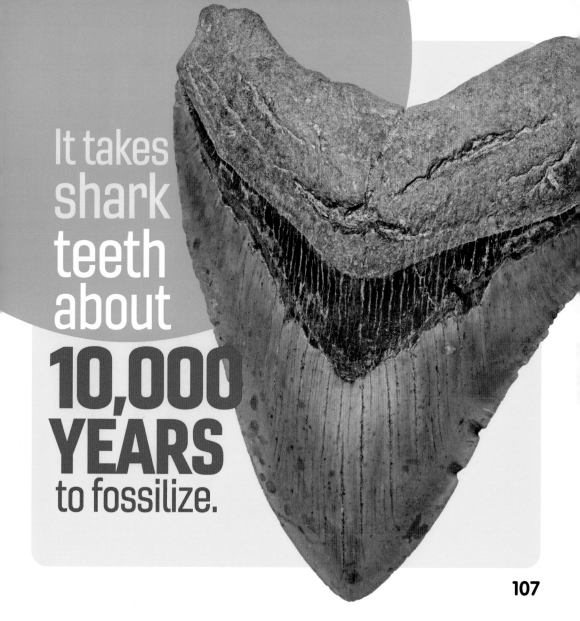

It takes shark teeth about **10,000 YEARS** to fossilize.

In 2020, the **MONSTER TRUCK MEGALODON** jumped over eight other Monster Jam trucks— **A WORLD RECORD.**

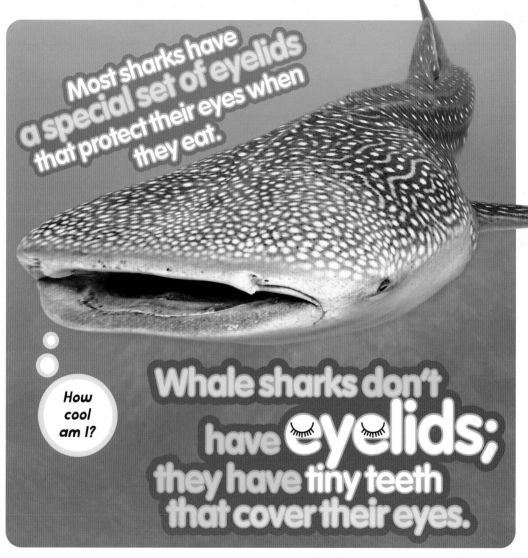

Most sharks have a special set of eyelids that protect their eyes when they eat.

How cool am I?

Whale sharks don't have eyelids; they have tiny teeth that cover their eyes.

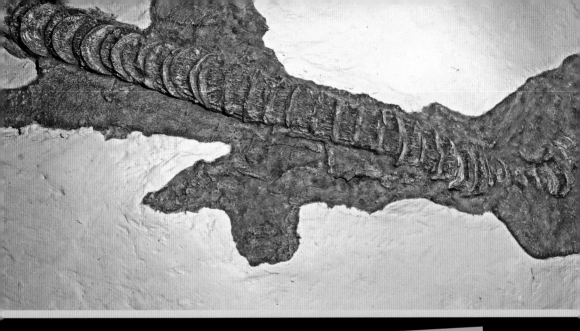

The **NINJA LANTERNSHARK** emits **a faint glow** that allows it to blend in with the **OCEAN'S LOW LIGHT** and sneak up on prey.

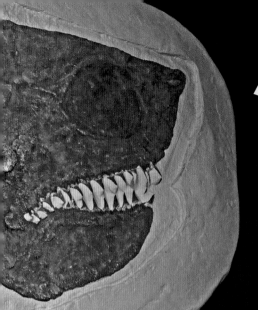

The **extinct "ginsu"** shark was nicknamed for a brand of **sharp chopping knives** after scientists found fossil evidence that it **sliced its prey into pieces.**

Its stealth moves inspired the **eight-year-old cousins** of the scientist who discovered the shark to come up with its **common name.**

USING **TRASH** FOUND **ON THE** BEACH, SUCH AS **BOTTLE CAPS,** TOILET SEATS, AND **TOYS,**

Now that's turning trash into treasure!

AN ARTIST CREATED A GREAT WHITE SHARK SCULPTURE NAMED GRETA.

Tiger sharks swim in **large loops** as they search for prey.

I'm getting dizzy...

You can use white modeling chocolate, sugar cubes, and marshmallows to make teeth for a shark cake.

115

The Smithsonian National Museum of Natural History has a

FULL-SIZE

MODEL

of A FEMALE

MEGALODON

hanging in its café.

A newborn great white shark is as long as a bathtub.

A newborn whale shark is about as long as a skateboard.

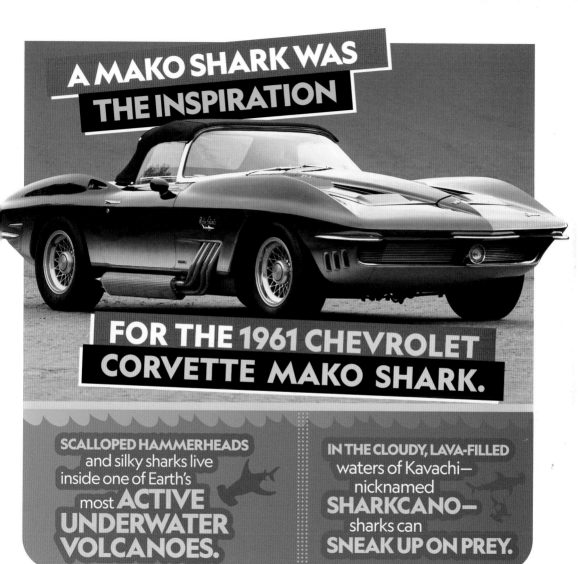

A MAKO SHARK WAS THE INSPIRATION

FOR THE 1961 CHEVROLET CORVETTE MAKO SHARK.

SCALLOPED HAMMERHEADS and silky sharks live inside one of Earth's most **ACTIVE UNDERWATER VOLCANOES.**

IN THE CLOUDY, LAVA-FILLED waters of Kavachi—nicknamed **SHARKCANO**—sharks can **SNEAK UP ON PREY.**

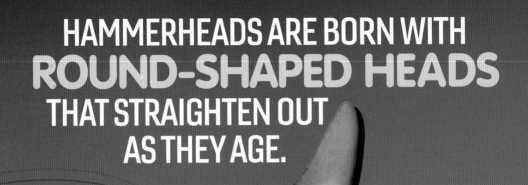

HAMMERHEADS ARE BORN WITH
ROUND-SHAPED HEADS
THAT STRAIGHTEN OUT
AS THEY AGE.

HAMMERHEAD SHARKS OFTEN SWIM TILTED TO ONE SIDE—AN ENERGY-EFFICIENT MANEUVER.

THE MECHANICAL SHARK IN THE MOVIE *JAWS* WAS 25 FEET (7.6 m) LONG AND WEIGHED ABOUT A TON (1t).

PYGMY RIBBONTAIL CAT SHARKS ARE ABOUT THE LENGTH OF A PIECE OF TOAST.

When people first settled in Iceland around A.D. 1000, they snacked on fermented Greenland sharks.

Great white sharks grow about

10

inches (25 cm) a year until they reach adulthood.

They made *hákarl,* or "rotten shark," by burying the sharks in sand for months.

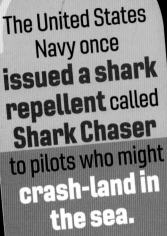

The United States Navy once **issued a shark repellent** called **Shark Chaser** to pilots who might **crash-land in the sea.**

Shark Chaser
was **a pink pill** that, when dropped in water, **released black ink** to **hide** the pilots in the ocean.

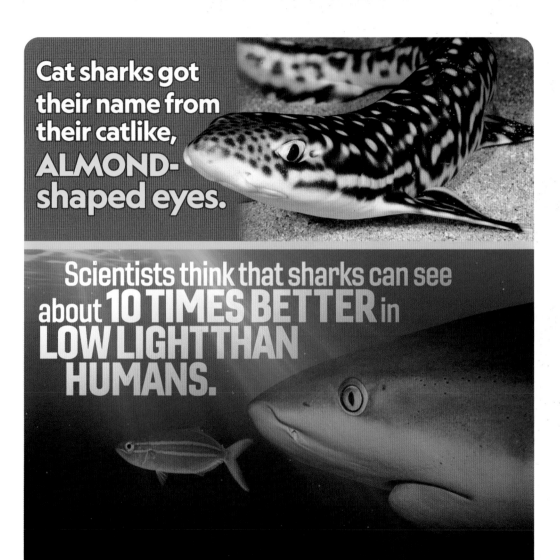

Cat sharks got their name from their catlike, **ALMOND-shaped eyes.**

Scientists think that sharks can see about **10 TIMES BETTER** in **LOW LIGHT THAN HUMANS.**

HORN SHARKS **HAVE A** HORNLIKE RIDGE OVER EACH EYE.

A MAKO SHARK CAN SWIM THE LENGTH OF ONE AND A HALF SCHOOL BUSES IN ONE SECOND.

GREAT WHITE SHARK ATTACKS ON HUMANS ARE OFTEN "SAMPLE BITES" the sharks release, rather than prey on, people.

When on the attack, salmon sharks swim in tight circles around schools of their prey. Pacific salmon being one of their favorite foods.

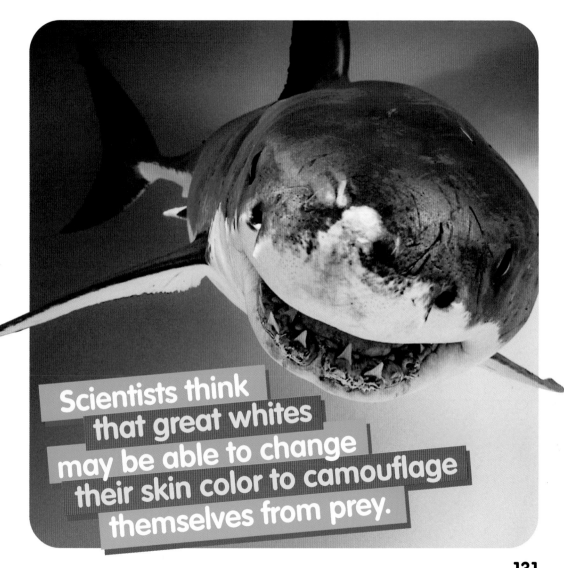

Scientists think that great whites may be able to change their skin color to camouflage themselves from prey.

The prehistoric male **FALCATUS** shark had a **SWORDLIKE FIN** on the top of its **HEAD.**

ONLY THE UPPER TEETH of the snaggletooth shark have **JAGGED EDGES,** which is why its scientific name means **"HALF SAW."**

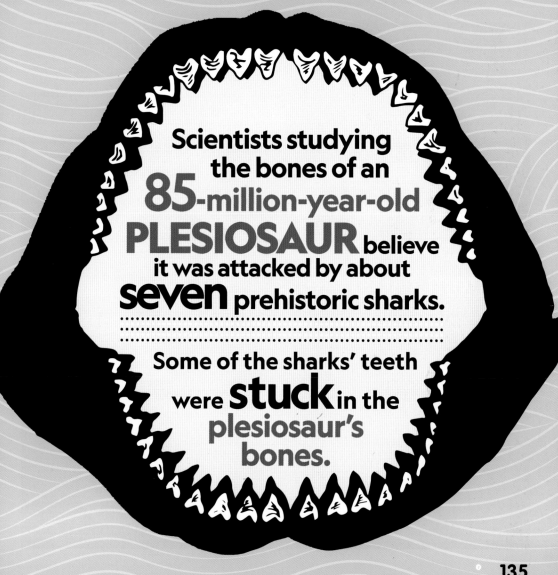

Scientists studying the bones of an **85**-million-year-old **PLESIOSAUR** believe it was attacked by about **seven** prehistoric sharks.

Some of the sharks' teeth were **stuck** in the plesiosaur's bones.

135

Blue sharks are known for stealing fish from fishermen's nets.

Nothing to see here.

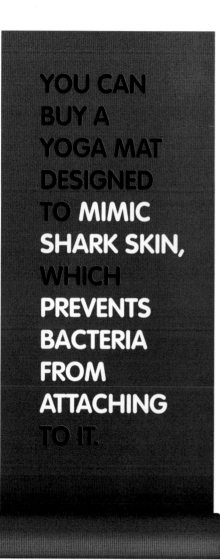

YOU CAN BUY A YOGA MAT DESIGNED TO **MIMIC SHARK SKIN,** WHICH PREVENTS BACTERIA FROM ATTACHING TO IT.

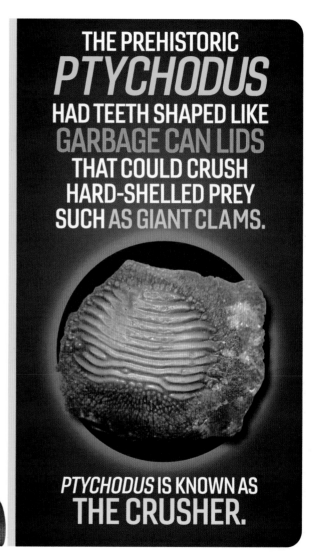

THE PREHISTORIC
PTYCHODUS
HAD TEETH SHAPED LIKE
GARBAGE CAN LIDS
THAT COULD CRUSH
HARD-SHELLED PREY
SUCH AS GIANT CLAMS.

PTYCHODUS IS KNOWN AS
THE CRUSHER.

AT AN
ART GALLERY
IN MARATHON,
FLORIDA, U.S.A.,
THERE ARE STAIRS
THAT ALLOW VISITORS
TO **CLIMB
INSIDE NIBBLES
THE SHARK'S
HEAD.**

The frilled shark can
SWALLOW PREY HALF ITS SIZE.

Fossilized shark teeth can be **WHITE, BROWN,** or **BLACK**—or even **BLUE.**

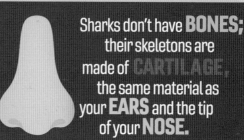

Sharks don't have **BONES;** their skeletons are made of **CARTILAGE,** the same material as your **EARS** and the tip of your **NOSE.**

Spiny dogfish **CURL UP** so that they can use **TWO SHARP SPINES** in front of their dorsal fins to **SLASH AT PREDATORS.**

The music that plays when the shark appears in *Jaws* consists of just two pairs of alternating notes—E and F or F and F sharp.

What a treat!

When great white sharks **poop,** a swarm of small fish follow to **eat the huge amount of waste.**

Divers swim in the **ICE-COVERED TOBOL RIVER** in Siberia to search for **FOSSILIZED SHARK TEETH.**

PYJAMA SHARKS curl into a ball if they FEEL THREATENED.

143

A DIVER IN FLORIDA, U.S.A., TOOK A PHOTO OF A **LEMON SHARK** WITH A **TOOTHY GRIN** JUST LIKE **BRUCE,** THE SHARK FROM **FINDING NEMO.**

145

Sharks have fin-gerprints— UNIQUE NOTCHES and RIDGES along their fins' edges that RESEARCHERS use to IDENTIFY INDIVIDUALS.

ABOUT **75** "SHARK CAMS" OFF THE COAST OF NORTH CAROLINA, U.S.A., **LET YOU WATCH LIVE SHARK ACTIVITY ONLINE.**

A SHARK-EYE CAMERA LETS RESEARCHERS **SEE HOW GLOWING SHARKS** APPEAR TO ONE ANOTHER.

The prehistoric **"EAGLE" SHARK'S** fins spanned nearly **six feet** (2 m) from tip to tip.

147

A researcher taught **captive lemon sharks** to **blink** when **a light flashed**— a skill they mastered **10 times faster** than cats.

148

Sharks have an **S-shaped heart** and a **U-shaped stomach.**

Venice, Florida, U.S.A., has been called the **"SHARK TOOTH CAPITAL OF THE WORLD"** because so many shark teeth **WASH UP ON ITS SHORES.**

You can rent a **SPECIAL SHOVEL IN VENICE** that lets you sift through sand to **FIND FOSSILS.**

DURING THE 19TH CENTURY, **PACIFIC ISLANDERS**

USED **SWORDS** AND **DAGGERS** WITH **SHARK TEETH** ALONG THE BLADES.

149

Young tiger sharks have **STRIPES THAT FADE** as they get older.

YOUNG GREAT WHITE SHARKS HAVE **WEAKER BITES** THAN ADULTS BECAUSE THE **CARTILAGE** IN THEIR JAWS HASN'T HARDENED YET.

The nervous shark **HIDES IN THE SEAGRASS** in mangrove forests.

Lemon sharks can detect one drop of tuna juice in 25 million drops of seawater.

SPYHOPPING

WHEN GREAT WHITE SHARKS POP THEIR HEADS ABOVE WATER TO LOOK FOR PREY

The **winghead shark** has the
widest head
of all hammerheads—
the width is about half

as long as the shark's
body length.

Pygmy sharks swim up from the ocean floor to **feed at night,** a round-trip distance of nearly **a mile** (1.6 km).

THE "POCKETS"
near the pectoral fins of
pocket sharks release a
GLOWING SUBSTANCE
they may use
FOR DEFENSE.

TYLOSAURUS,
A MARINE REPTILE
CONSIDERED ONE OF THE
DEADLIEST
HUNTERS

IN **PREHISTORIC SEAS,** DINED ON SHARKS.

A HOUSE IN OXFORD, ENGLAND, HAS A **26-FOOT** (8-m)**-LONG SHARK** MODEL THAT LOOKS LIKE **IT CRASHED INTO THE ROOF.**

Cookiecutter sharks shed **their lower teeth** and then swallow them.

CLEANER WRASSE FISH

SWIM INTO SHARKS' MOUTHS TO

EAT UNSWALLOWED **FOOD.**

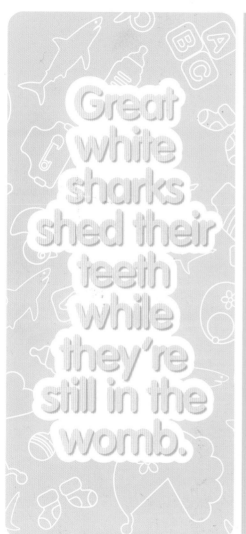

Great white sharks shed their teeth while they're still in the womb.

PUFFADDER SHYSHARKS *curl up*

in a circle and use their tails to cover **THEIR HEADS.**

Spiny dogfish sharks travel and hunt in packs like **dogs**—that's how they got **their** name.

In 2005, scientists discovered that a **great** white shark swam from South Africa to Australia and back again in almost a straight line.

AUSTRALIA

SOUTH AFRICA

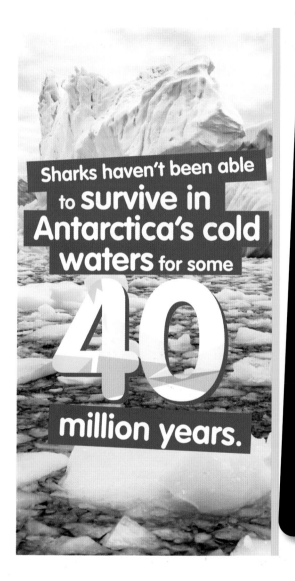

Sharks haven't been able to **survive in Antarctica's cold waters** for some **40** million years.

In 2013, more than **40,000 PEOPLE** on social media followed **LYDIA,** the first great white shark ever recorded **to cross the Atlantic Ocean.**

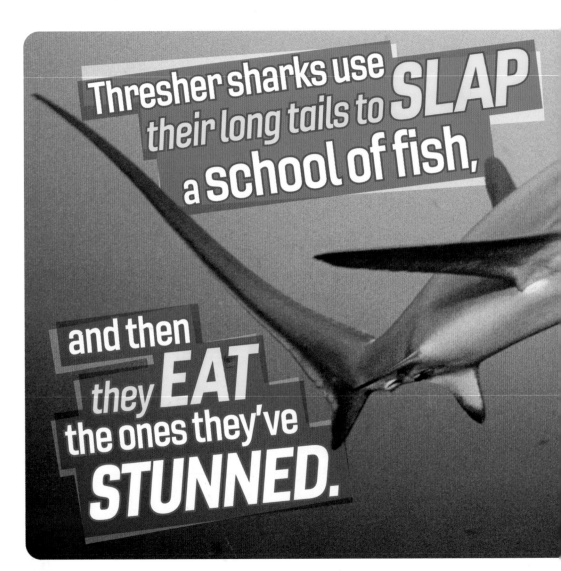

Thresher sharks use their long tails to **SLAP** a **school of fish,** and then they **EAT** the ones they've **STUNNED.**

A thresher shark's **tail** can be **as long as the rest of its body.**

Baby lemon sharks **swim in** flooded mangrove "nurseries" that are only **knee-high.**

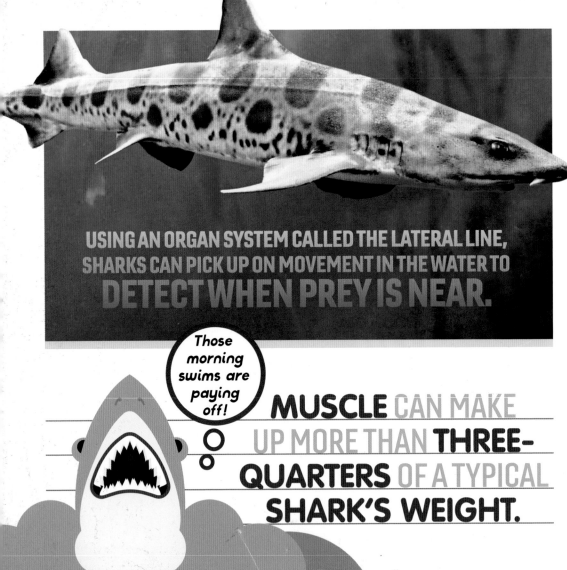

USING AN ORGAN SYSTEM CALLED THE LATERAL LINE, SHARKS CAN PICK UP ON MOVEMENT IN THE WATER TO DETECT WHEN PREY IS NEAR.

Those morning swims are paying off!

MUSCLE CAN MAKE UP MORE THAN THREE-QUARTERS OF A TYPICAL SHARK'S WEIGHT.

Most **shark fossils** are **teeth.**

Shark skin feels like **sandpaper** when rubbed from **tail** to head.

FEMALE LEMON SHARKS return to where they were born to GIVE BIRTH TO THEIR PUPS.

An octopus can use its arms to **COVER THE GILLS** of a PYJAMA SHARK, **starving the predator of OXYGEN.**

Sharks can see the color yellow especially well.

Shark researchers jokingly refer to the bright yellow color often found on flotation devices as "YUM-YUM YELLOW."

The draughtsboard shark gulps air, which makes a **BARK-LIKE SOUND** when released.

You too, huh?

Some great white sharks **move their bodies** in an **S shape** when they **poop.**

A shark's eyes shine in the dark, like a cat's.

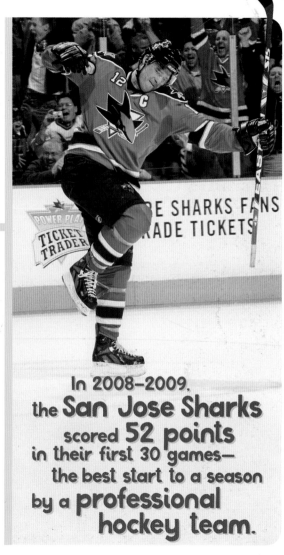

If your mouth were as comparatively large as a megamouth's, it would be **a foot** (30 cm) **wide.**

In 2008–2009, the **San Jose Sharks** scored **52 points** in their first 30 games— the best start to a season by a **professional hockey team.**

Some sharks **can survive** for several hours out of water.

Swell sharks **gulp water** and **balloon** to twice their normal size to protect themselves.

MORE THAN THREE-QUARTERS OF SHARK SPECIES WILL RARELY **SEE A HUMAN OR ARE UNABLE TO EAT HUMANS.**

The massive "Planet Ocean" mural in Long Beach, California, U.S.A., features life-size sharks.

It took **7,000** gallons (26,500 L) of paint to create the **1,280**-foot (390-m)-**long mural.**

Scientists got a great white shark to **swallow a tracking device** by **wrapping it in seal fat,** which they called

A BLUBBER BURRITO.

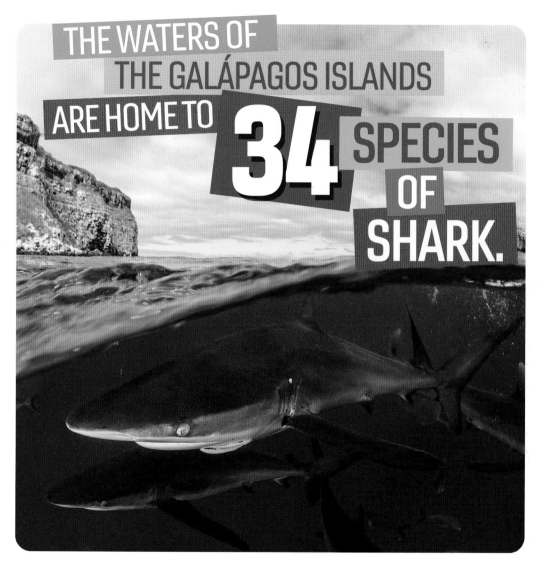

THE WATERS OF THE GALÁPAGOS ISLANDS ARE HOME TO **34** SPECIES OF SHARK.

Olympic swimmers have worn swimsuits modeled on shark skin.

Hello, little friends!

A whale shark can weigh about as

Swimmers at an underwater park in Palm Beach County, Florida, U.S.A., can snorkel around three **1,500-pound (680-kg) hammerhead statues.**

much as five large African elephants.

At the **ALBUQUERQUE INTERNATIONAL BALLOON FIESTA** in New Mexico, U.S.A., **a shark-shaped hot-air balloon** took to the **SKIES.**

Most female sharks lose their appetite before giving birth, which prevents them from eating their own pups.

THE INSIDE OF **A MEGAMOUTH SHARK'S MOUTH GLOWS** TO **ATTRACT PREY.**

SHARKS IN AQUARIUMS ARE KNOWN TO SPIT OUT THEIR VITAMINS.

Each tooth in the ANCIENT CLADODONT SHARK'S mouth had A SINGLE SPIKE

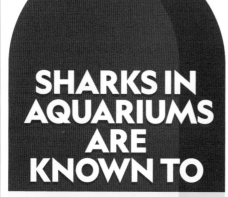

surrounded by smaller SPIKES.

Sharks range in **size** from the length of a **pencil** to a **SCHOOL BUS.**

VISITORS WHO STAND BY A GIANT SHARK MURAL IN ST. PETERSBURG, FLORIDA, U.S.A., LOOK LIKE THEY ARE ABOUT TO GET CHOMPED.

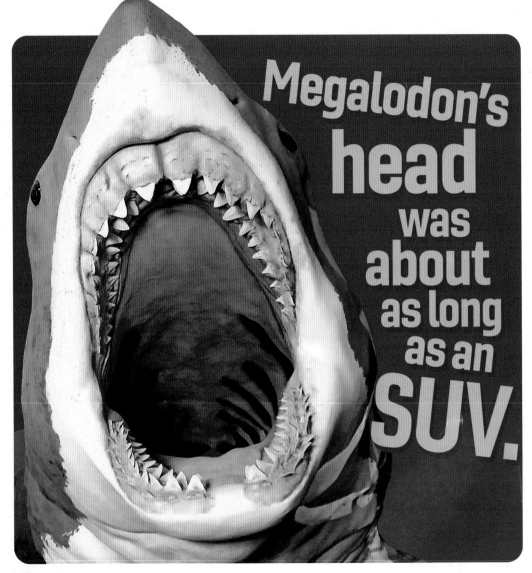

Megalodon's head was about as long as an SUV.

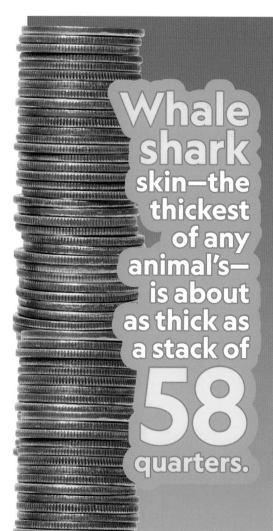

Whale shark skin—the thickest of any animal's— is about as thick as a stack of

58

quarters.

An ancient Hawaiian legend tells of a kind shark that **left food** on the beach every day for an **elderly couple** to **eat.**

More than **100** SPECIES OF SHARK swim off the coast of **SOUTH AFRICA.**

ATLANTIC OCEAN

EUROPE

ASIA

AFRICA

ATLANTIC OCEAN

INDIAN OCEAN

0   1,000 miles
0   1,000 kilometers

NUMBER OF SHARK SPECIES
60–105
36–59
1–35
0

Swordfish sometimes kill sharks with their

LONG, POINTED BILLS.

Bull sharks have traveled up the Mississippi River as far north as St. Louis, Missouri, U.S.A.

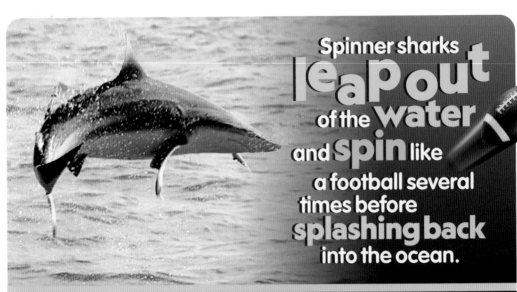

Spinner sharks **leaP oUt** of the **water** and **spin** like a football several times before **splashing back** into the ocean.

ANGEL SHARKS SOMETIMES sit camouflaged on the seafloor for days, STRIKING WHEN PREY SWIMS BY.

Hush! I'm hiding.

Shortfin makos can leap 30 FEET (9 m) out of the water— that's as tall as a three-story building.

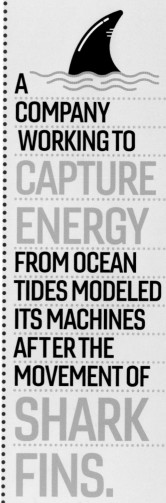

A COMPANY WORKING TO CAPTURE ENERGY FROM OCEAN TIDES MODELED ITS MACHINES AFTER THE MOVEMENT OF SHARK FINS.

THE MAKO ROLLER COASTER

AT SEAWORLD IN ORLANDO, FLORIDA, U.S.A.,

REACHES SPEEDS

FASTER THAN A CAR ON A HIGHWAY.

Greenland sharks have **compounds in their bodies** that act like a **natural antifreeze,** allowing them to swim in the **Arctic's cold waters.**

The molecules that cause some sharks to **GLOW GREEN** may also help protect them from diseases.

During the late Cretaceous, part of what is today Alabama, U.S.A., was underwater and a hotbed for *SHARKS.*

Horn sharks use their **pelvic fins** to scoot along the **ocean floor.**

193

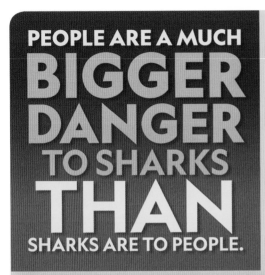

PEOPLE ARE A MUCH **BIGGER DANGER** TO SHARKS **THAN** SHARKS ARE TO PEOPLE.

Sharks have **INTERNAL EARS.**

Cat sharks not only **glow**—they glow in **specific patterns.**

Artist Damien Hirst **created a work** that displayed a *PRESERVED DEAD TIGER SHARK* in a **GLASS CASE.**

Shark poop is **YELL⊙W-GREEN.**

THRESHER SHARKS CAN WHIP THEIR TAILS AT PREY AS FAST AS **80 MILES AN HOUR** (129 km/h).

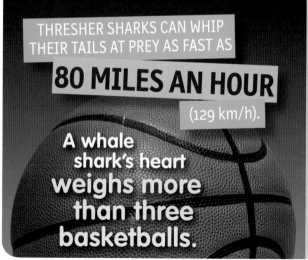

A whale shark's heart weighs more than three basketballs.

THE CONSTELLATION **BAIDAM,** MADE UP OF THE STARS IN THE BIG DIPPER, IS **SHAPED LIKE A SHARK.**

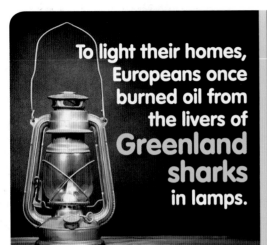

To light their homes, Europeans once burned oil from the livers of **Greenland sharks** in lamps.

HORN SHARKS INJECT VENOM
INTO PREDATORS BY USING TWO SHORT HORNS IN FRONT OF THEIR DORSAL FINS.

Blue sharks are named for the **unique color of their skin.**

An ancient shark nicknamed the "GODZILLA" SHARK had 12 ROWS OF SHARP TEETH.

In the movie *Deep Blue Sea,* filmmakers used equipment found in **airplanes** to create the animatronic mako shark.

SCIENTISTS IN NOVA SCOTIA, CANADA, TAGGED A **17-FOOT** (5.2-m)-LONG, **3,541-POUND** (1,606-kg) GREAT WHITE SHARK THEY CALL **"QUEEN OF THE OCEAN."**

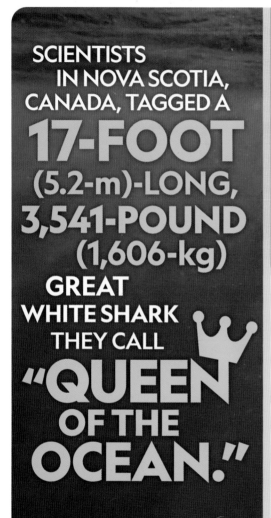

Golfers putt alongside about **12 BULL SHARKS** that live in a lake on a Queensland, Australia, golf course.

Archaeologists discovered the **3,000-year-old skeletal** remains of a man attacked **by a shark in Japan.**

Researchers **MEASURE** extinct sharks' fossilized **TEETH** to **ESTIMATE** the **ANIMALS' SIZE.**

Boldface indicates illustrations.

Since 1888, the National Geographic Society has funded more than 14,000 research, conservation, education, and storytelling projects around the world. National Geographic Partners distributes a portion of the funds it receives from your purchase to National Geographic Society to support programs including the conservation of animals and their habitats. To learn more, visit natgeo.com/info.

For more information, visit nationalgeographic .com, call 1-877-873-6846, or write to the following address:

National Geographic Partners, LLC
1145 17th Street NW
Washington, DC 20036-4688 U.S.A.

For librarians and teachers: nationalgeographic.com/ books/librarians-and-educators

More for kids from National Geographic: natgeokids.com

National Geographic Kids magazine inspires children to explore their world with fun yet educational articles on animals, science, nature, and more. Using fresh storytelling and amazing photography, *Nat Geo Kids* shows kids ages 6 to 14 the fascinating truth about the world—and why they should care. **natgeo.com/subscribe**

For rights or permissions inquiries, please contact National Geographic Books Subsidiary Rights: bookrights@natgeo.com

The publisher would like to thank the fin-tastic book team: Michelle Harris and Julie Beer, writers; Grace Hill and Kathryn Williams, editors; Julide Dengel, designer; Sarah Mock, photo editor; Robin Palmer, researcher; Molly Reid, production editor; and Gus Tello, designer.

Trade paperback ISBN: 978-1-4263-7240-7
Reinforced library binding ISBN: 978-1-4263-7241-4

Printed in China
22/PPS/1

PHOTO CREDITS

AL = Alamy Stock Photo; AS = Adobe Stock; GI = Getty Images; SS = Shutterstock

Cover (UP CTR), Sean/AS;(UP RT), Doug Perrine/Nature Picture Library; (LO RT), Andy Murch/Image Quest Marine;(LO LE), EXTREME-PHOTOGRAPHER/GI;(CTR LE), Wildestanimal/AL; Spine, Wildestanimal/AL; Back Cover, bullet_chained/AS; 1 (BACKGROUND), Romolo Tavani/AS; 2-3 (BACKGROUND), Romolo Tavani/AS; 2, wildestanimal/AS; 3, Sergey Uryadnikov/Dreamstime; 4 (BACKGROUND), bayqpatterns/SS; 4 (UP LE), hanahusain/SS; 4 (dog), Kimberly Reinick/AS; 4 (hat), Aleksangel/SS; 4 (RT), Andrea Izzotti/AS; 5 (LE), Fiona Ayerst/SS; 5 (LO RT), Will Schubert/Blue Planet Archive; 6-7, Krzysztof Odziomek/Dreamstime; 6-7 (fingerprints), Andrey Kuzmin/AS; 8, Mike Price/SS; 8-9 (CTR), bekirevren/AS; 9, wildestanimal/AS; 10, Franco Tempesta; 11 (LE), Doug Perrine/Blue Planet Archive; 11 (RT), HollyHarry/AS; 12 (UP), Ethan Daniels/Blue Planet Archive; 12 (LO), muchmania/AS; 13, frantisekhojdysz/SS; 14, wildestanimal/GI; 15 (UP), Makoto Hirose/e-Photo/Blue Planet Archive; 15 (LO LE), toricheks/AS; 15 (LO RT), Dmitry Kalinovsky/SS; 16-17, Shane Gross/Nature Picture Library; 18 (UP), Jeff Milisen/Blue Planet Archive; 18 (LO), wildestanimal/AS; 19 (CTR LE), Jerome Mallefet; 19 (LO RT), Eric Isselée/AS; 19 (LO CTR), Samantha Leigh, PhD; 20 (UP), dottedyeti/AS; 20 (LO), oxyggen/AS; 21, wildestanimal/AS; 22 (UP), Sabine/AS; 22 (LO), MicroOne/SS; 23, Veronika Surovtseva/SS; 24-25, the Ocean Agency/AS; 26, David B. Fleetham/Blue Planet Archive; 26 (CTR LE), Happypictures/AS; 27, Alhovik/Dreamstime; 28, Happy monkey/AS; 29 (LE), Jelger Herder/Buiten-Beeld/AL; 29 (BACKGROUND), gepard/AS; 29 (RT), natrot/AS; 30 (LE), maryartist/SS; 30 (RT), Irina K./AS; 31 (UP LE), klyaksun/AS; 31 (shark), Yves Lefèvre/Biosphoto; 31 (LO RT), Zebra Finch/AS; 31 (LO LE), 2DAssets/SS; 32 (UP), NG Maps; 32 (LO), jonnysek/AS; 33 (UP), Michael Woodruff/SS; 34-35 (BACKGROUND), Kundra/AS; 34-35 (CTR), NG Maps; 34 (UP), Eric Isselée/AS; 34 (LO), zimagine/AS; 35 (UP), AvetPhotos/SS; 35 (LO), Rich Carey/SS; 36-37, wildestanimal/AS; 37 (LO LE), timtimphoto/AS; 37 (RT), Breck P. Kent/SS; 38, Mr. Yoshi; 39, Esteban De Armas/SS; 40, Andy Murch/Image Quest Marine; 41 (UP), yekaterinalim/AS; 41 (LO), Erin Dillon & Jorge Ceballos; 42, Mauricio Handler/GI; 43, VisionDiveAS; 46 (ball), Willard/GI; 44-45, Tomas Kotouc/SS; 46 (LO), Greg Lovett/Palm Beach Post/ZUMAPRESS; 47, Lana/AS; 48 (UP), Adam/AS; 48 (LO RT), Annity Art/SS; 48 (LO LE), GalapagosPhoto/SS; 49, Bruce Rasner/Blue Planet Archive; 50 (BACKGROUND), augustus/SS; 50 (CTR), Olga Lebedeva/SS; 50 (shark), Magic world of design/SS; 51 (UP), Alex Mustard/Nature Picture Library; 51 (LO RT), Design Studio RM/AS; 51 (calendar), Jane Kelly/AS; 51 (icon), Eriska melody/AS; 52 (UP), Kelvin Aitken/VWPics/AL; 52 (LO), wildestanimal/SS; 54-55, TRIPPLAAR KRISTOFFER/SIPA/Newscom; 56 (UP), Westend61/GI; 57 (UP), estudio Maia/SS; 56-57 (LO), Joe Belanger/SS; 58, Mauricio Alvarez Abel; 59, Shane Gross/Nature Picture Library; 59 (masks), sudowoodo/AS; 60, Franco Tempesta; 61, Papilio/AL; 62 (UP), Red Monkey/AS; 63 (UP), RanMarine; 62-63 (LO), David Gruber; 64 (UP), cherylvb/AS; 64 (LO), lukaspuchrik/AS; 65, Andy Murch/Image Quest Marine; 66 (BACKGROUND), whitcomberd/AS; 66, Ken Kiefer 2/GI; 67 (RT), cherylvb/AS; 67 (LE), Andrey_Kuzmin/SS; 68-69, Grant M Henderson/SS; 70 (UP), Dr. Stepnen Goafrey/Calvert Marine Museum; 70 (LO LE), Tom/AS; 70 (LO RT), mark/AS; 71, Klaus Jost/Blue Planet Archive; 72 (LE), Atlantis Paradise Island/Mega/Newscom; 72 (CTR), Jochen Tack/AL; 73 (LE), primopiano/SS; 73 (RT), Bambang TJ/SS; 74-75 (ALL), Universal Pictures/Photofest; 76 (UP), Masa Ushioda/Blue Planet Archive; 76 (LO LE), Pavel Talashov/SS; 77 (UP), Alessandro De Maddalena/GI; 77 (LO), Afanasia/AS; 78, Noel/AS; 78 (INSET), Fernando Astasio Avila/SS; 79 (UP), Tsado/AS; 79 (LO RT), endstern/AS; 79 (LO LE), Doug Perrine/Nature Picture Library; 80, Kovalenko I/AS; 81, Annity Art/SS; 82, Sergey Uryadnikov/SS; 83 (UP LE), Olga_i/SS; 83 (LO LE), preto_perola/AS; 83 (RT), fotoyou/AS; 84-85, Michael Bogner/AS; 86 (UP), bergamont/SS; 86 (LO), ratpack223/AS; 86 (diver), ashva73/AS; 87 (UP), Doug Perrine/Blue Planet Archive; 87 (LO RT), cookiechoo/AS; 87 (LO LE), Jessica/AS; 88-89 (UP), Makoto Kubo/e-Photo/Blue Planet Archive; 88 (LO), Eric Isselee/SS; 89 (LO), Alex Mustard/Nature Picture Library; 90, Walt Disney Studios Motion Pictures/Photofest; 91 (LE), Doug Perrine/Blue Planet Archive; 91 (UP RT), percom/SS; 91 (LO RT),

SBS Eclectic Images/AL; 92 (UP), Fiona Ayerst/SS; 92 (LO), olando/AS; 93, Andy Murch/Blue Planet Archive; 94 (UP), Rich Carey/SS; 94 (bones), Titima Ongkantong/SS; 94 (LO), nerthuz/AS; 95, Artur/AS; 95 (pacifier), Farah Sadikhova/SS; 97 (LE), Brandelet/SS; 97 (RT), topvectors/AS; 98-99 (UP), MR1805/GI; 98 (LO), JIANG HONGYAN/SS; 99 (LO LE), focus_bell/AS; 99 (LO RT), liloocola/AS; 100-101, Kelvin Aitken/V&W/Image Quest Marine; 102, Dendy Harya/SS; 103 (LE), Zoonar/Galyna Andrushko/AL; 103 (RT), (Joaquín Espinoza); 104, wildestanimal/SS; 105 (UP), Daniel Hernanz Ramos/GI; 105 (LO RT), Soulartist/SS; 105 (LO LE), Supza/SS; 106, Mark Witton; 107, Mark_Kostich/SS; 108, Paulo Lopes/Zuma Wire; 109, Krzysztof Odziomek/Dreamstime; 110 (UP), Millard H. Sharp/Science Source; 110 (LO), Vicky Vasquez; 112-113, Washed Ashore; 112-113 (trash cans), antto/AS; 114, yoshinori/AS; 115 (BACKGROUND), paketesama/AS; 115 (LE), Q77photo/AS; 115 (RT), Cindy Ord/GI; 116-117, John Whitaker; 118 (UP), Nerthuz/SS; 118 (CTR), Nomadsoul1/Dreamstime; 118 (LO), Evikka/SS; 119 (UP), Uli Jooss/culture-images GmbH/AL; 119 (LO), Alfmaler/SS; 120, Martin Strmiska/AL; 121, Universal Pictures/Photofest; 122 (UP), prochym/AS; 122 (LO), Masa Ushioda/Blue Planet Archive; 122 (eyes), 2DAssets/SS; 123 (toast), Alexstar/Dreamstime; 123 (CTR), Roberto Nistri/AL; 124-125 (UP), ramoncarretero/AS; 124-125 (LO), Elmiral/SS; 126 (pill), Ayseliani/AS; 126 (INSET), Jessica/AS; 127 (UP), SergeUWPhoto/SS; 127 (water), vchalup/AS; 127 (LO), timsimages/AS; 128, Timmothy Mcdade/SS; 129, Darin Sakdatorn/AS; 130, Vladyslav Travel photo/SS; 131, David B. Fleetham/Blue Planet Archive; 132-133, Franco Tempesta; 134, Matthew Oldfield, ScubaZoo/Science Source; 135, Alexey Vorobyov/AS; 136 (BACKGROUND), Darien Sanchez/AS; 136 (LO), prochym/AS; 137 (LE), happyvector071/AS; 137 (RT), Sabena Jane Blackbird/AL; 138, Barry Gaukel; 139 (UP), sam/AS; 139 (LO), Panda Vector/SS; 140, Andy Murch/Nature Picture Library; 141, topvectors/AS; 142 (UP), Willyam Bradberry/SS; 142 (CTR), murphy81/AS; 143, Cheryl-Samantha Owen/Nature Picture Library; 144-145, KW MacWilliams/Caters News Agency; 146, Uryadnikov Sergey/AS; 147 (UP), artjazz/SS; 147 (INSET), Janos/AS; 148, Drew/AS; 148 (flashlights), Moises Fernandez/SS; 148 (LO), Pavel Timofeev/SS; 149 (CTR LE), I. Pilon/SS; 149 (CTR RT), Werner Forman Archive/SS; 150, le breuil baptiste/SS; 151 (LO), viktorijareut/AS; 152-153, prochym/AS; 154 (UP), Shengyong Li/SS; 154 (LO RT), zimagine/AS; 154 (LO LE), Marta/AS; 155 (UP), Stephen Kajiura/Blue Planet Archive; 155 (LO LE), Anita Ponne/SS; 155 (stars), Foxyliam/SS; 156-157, Mohamad Haghani/Stocktrek Images/GI; 158 (UP), Alex Robinson/robertharding/AL; 158 (LO), Doug Perrine/AL; 159, David Fleetham/Nature Picture Library; 160, Stephen Frink/GI; 161 (LE), Jan Engel/AS; 161 (RT), Doug Perrine/Blue Planet Archive; 162 (UP), Andy Murch/Blue Planet Archive; 162 (LO), EreborMountain/SS; 163 (LE), Song_about_summer/AS; 164, Amos Nachoum/Blue Planet Archive; 165, Tom/AS; 166 (UP), Barbara Ash/SS; 166 (LO), popaukropa/AS; 167 (LE), Gerry Bishop/SS; 167 (UP RT), TextureMaster/AS; 168-169, kondratuk/AS; 170, Claudio Divizia/AS; 171 (UP), Alex Mustard/Nature Picture Library; 171 (LO), Viorel Sima/SS; 172, wildestanimal/GI; 173 (UP LE), TRAVELARIUM; 173 (LO LE), Margaret/AS; 173 (RT), Don Smith/GI; 174 (UP), Doug Perrine/Blue Planet Archive; 174 (LO), Mark Conlin/Blue Planet Archive; 175 (shark), Tom/AS; 176 (LE), Jeff Gritchen/Digital First Media/Orange County Register via GI; 176 (RT), mix3r/AS; 177, Bernard Radvaner/GI; 178 (UP), FRANCOIS-XAVIER MARIT/AFP via GI; 178 (LO), Yuliia/AS; 179 (UP), Richard Graulich/The Palm Beach Post via Zuma Press; 179 (LO), Richard Peterson/SS; 178-179 (scale), gearstd/AS; 180, Efrain Padro/AL; 181, kelttt/AS; 182, Tom Haight/Blue Planet Archive; 183 (RT), Sterberg Museum of Natural History; 184 (sharks), Tom/AS; 184 (pencil), Pan Stock/SS; 184 (bus), Joy Brown/SS; 185, Sarah J. Mock; 186, Gil Cohiba/SS; 187 (LE), Hurst Photo/SS; 188 (UP), lunamarina/SS; 188 (LO LE), NG Maps; 190 (UP LE), Ronald C. Modra/GI; 190 (UP RT), mtsaride/AS; 190 (LO), LuisMiguel/AS; 191 (LE), Kharlamova/AS; 191 (CTR), Richard Ellis/Blue Planet Archive; 191 (UP RT), D-sign Studio 10/SS; 192, Viaval Tours/SS; 193 (LE), kilroy79/AS; 193 (CTR RT), archivector/AS; 194 (UP), guardiano007/SS; 194 (LO), David Gruber; 195, Skypixel/Dreamstime; 196 (UP), Zhanna/AS; 196 (LO), Samy Kassem/SS; 197, Jessie Pruitt/Buzzsaw Studio; 198, Warner Bros./Photofest; 199 (LE), Harry Collins/AS; 199 (crown), barks/AS; 199 (UP RT), dolimac/AS

HUNGRY FOR MORE SHARK STUFF?

NATIONAL GEOGRAPHIC KiDS

CAN'T GET ENOUGH

Shark Stuff

FUN FACTS, AWESOME INFO, COOL GAMES, SILLY JOKES, AND MORE!

WE GET IT.

That's why we made *Can't Get Enough Shark Stuff.* It's the perfect combination of facts, stories, photos, and fun all about the world's most ferocious and fascinating ocean predator.

NATIONAL GEOGRAPHIC KiDS

AVAILABLE WHEREVER BOOKS ARE SOLD

Discover more at natgeokids.com